The Recipe for Healing Love, Hope & Faith from a Deep Soul

Bro. Larry

Thanks for supporting me. I appreciate you sowing seeds into my dream by helping to make my first book a success.

God Bless

Tony

The Recipe for Healing Love, Hope & Faith from a Deep Soul

Tonya LaShawn

Copyright © 2016 by Tonya Lowery.
Cover Art by Nicole D. Williamson
Make-up and Photography by Calique Smith

ISBN:	Softcover	978-1-5144-3924-1
	eBook	978-1-5144-3923-4

All rights reserved. No part of this book may be reproduced or transmitted in any form or by any means, electronic or mechanical, including photocopying, recording, or by any information storage and retrieval system, without permission in writing from the copyright owner.

BIBLE CITATIONS
Scripture quotations marked KJV are from the Holy Bible, King James Version (Authorized Version). First published in 1611. Quoted from the KJV Classic Reference Bible, Copyright © 1983 by The Zondervan Corporation.

Any people depicted in stock imagery provided by Thinkstock are models, and such images are being used for illustrative purposes only. Certain stock imagery © Thinkstock.

Print information available on the last page.

Rev. date: 01/06/2016

To order additional copies of this book, contact:
Xlibris
1-888-795-4274
www.Xlibris.com
Orders@Xlibris.com

Contents

Dedication vii
Acknowledgements ix

Chapter 1: Love 1

Single Mom 5
Love's Rhythm 9
When A Man Loves A Woman 11
What is Love? 13

Chapter 2: Hope 15

Life 19
When We Remembered 23
Anyway 27
Hope In A Time of Hidden Agendas 29

Chapter 3: Faith 33

Never Give Up 37
Jesus 41
Angels 43
Only a Prayer Away 45

Scriptural References 49

Dedication

I first of all dedicate this book to my mother Eleanor Lowery and my deceased grandmother Grace Humphries. My Mom has always been my biggest cheerleader and at times my biggest critic. Thanks for giving me tough love when I needed it the most because it prepared me for life's adversities. Between you and grandma growing up was pretty interesting but I'm glad I was raised by two strong women because you two prepared me for life. I'd also like to thank my brother, aunts, as well as other loved ones and you know who you are for your continued love and support. I thank God every day for you all.

Acknowledgements

I'd first like to give honor and thanks to God because apart from him I can do nothing. I give thanks to my sister and brother circle for being there for me in so many ways during my trying storms of life. I'd also like to thank my church family at Metropolitan Wesley A.M.E. Zion church, especially to those members who have been my cheerleaders on the side lines of life. I'd like to thank you all along with family and friends for your loving words of encouragement, prayers, your love, and just for being there in my time of need. I love each and every one of you. You all hold a special place in my heart. I would list you all by name but the list is pretty long so I give thanks to God for putting my family, friends, church family, mentors, and strangers who were angels in disguise in my path. You all have made my life so much richer. May God continue to bless each and every one of you and may his peace be upon you. Glory be to God for the things he has done and will continue to do in my future!!!

Chapter 1

LOVE

Love is one of life's most splendid gifts that God has given us. God is love and his love can be seen in many ways or forms. The opposite of love is hate and God doesn't hate us but he hates the sin in us. None of us are exempted from it, we're born into it. Love is something that every human being needs and is one that is also miss- used, misunderstood, and at times can be painful. These circumstances are because of how man uses it but God's love is unconditional its agape love. Very few people really know how to love and they search for love in all the wrong places. One must first love God and themselves in order to love others. Unfortunely, some have experienced pain stemming first from their childhood, which causes them to retreat from others, build walls around their heart, or hurt others by not projecting love toward their spouses and mates. These problems from their childhood are because love was not shown in their household. They probably didn't have any other relatives to show them love either so, lack of intimacy gets carried over into their adulthood. It's been my observation in human nature that our childhood can sometimes dictate

our future if one chooses. Notice I stated sometimes. It can be changed through God's love, self-change, and in opening up your heart to the beautiful aspects of what real love has to offer. The operative word is **real** which means genuine, not fake or artificial. Real love is patient, kind, sacrificial, and doesn't keep score or boast. It also; frees your spirit. When you really love from the heart you just find yourself doing and going the extra mile for a person. It could be for your parents, your children, relatives, spouse, friends, mates, and even a pet. It becomes instinctive when one gives love and in reciprocating love back. These poems in this chapter will reflect just a few of love's characteristics. God is amazing in how he poured his love down to each of us so we can use it toward others. People say I love you and it's all so easy to utter the word from their lips, but their true love is proven when put to a test. Believe it or not love does conquer all. It's the God given weapon that does prosper. It can bring the strongest of men to his knees, it brings peace to a weary land, and forges forgiveness in broken relationships. Love is indeed a powerful potion when put into motion. It's like war easy to start but hard to finish.

Single Mom

It's 6am and I'm rolling out of bed, got to go to work cause the kids got to be fed plus bills got to get paid in order to maintain where we stay
Get to work and the boss is acting like a nasty fool
Co-workers scheming and deceiving with dagger looks in their eyes
But I gotta keep my head up, I refuse to be down so, I look to the heavens for my protection
Some brothas trippin cause I'm independent, strong, and not easily torn
But they gotta realize my kids come first before any smooth fast talking dude
They have to come correct and clean or else I'll have to be mean
I won't stand for any hidden agendas, fake me outs, or pretenders
To love me is to love my kids, that's the way it is and always will be
Love me or leave me, but don't spoon feed me
My kids are my heart and any man that tries to hurt them, I'll tear apart
So here's a word of advice to all women and single moms alike
Love yourself and be true to you to, real love will find you
A real man will take notice of your self- worth and see that you're a special kinda lady
Wait on the Lord, be a diamond in the ruff don't expect no crazy stuff, these traits will shine bright which will attract Mr. Right

- Take the time to know him, be alert to any red flags, God will tell you if he's worth while
- Build up the God in you, train up your kids in him cause, the hand that rocks the cradle rules the world, so raise your children with a nourishing, firm, and Godly hand, so they can be good leaders in their land.

Love's Rhythm

There are times when I am afraid
I feel defeated but I see a ray of light that slowly creeps on in
I see that my tomorrow has countless possibilities
I see the bright smiles from children's laughter that reflects signs of life's innocence
I see the beauty in nature when I hear the birds singing & chirping in the early morn
I see the waves of the ocean kiss the sandy shores
I see the sparks of hope in times of natural disasters
I see close knit friendships which are tied with loyalty instead of deceit
I see couples holding hands while walking in the park
I see communities building good relational bridges and employing businesses
I see seniors not being afraid to walk the streets or to speak
I see and hear lyrics in songs that ignite pleasant dreams and don't demean
Love's Rhythm has a prescribed order that's patient, gentle, kind, and oh so divine
When it's true it will be there for you, lasting throughout the test of time

When A Man Loves A Woman

When a man loves a woman he will treat her like a queen
When she is sick he will cater to her
When she is weary he will carry her load
When she is in emotional distress he
will try to ease her worries
When she needs shelter from the storm
he will wrap his arms around her
When she love he will comfort her
When she is lost he will be a light to God's pathway
He will have a vision to present to her
from God and from that union
God will birth a life of love that with stand
many of the world's strive, but that love will
be a fulfillment unto God's kingdom

What is Love?

Is love the connection of two hearts that embrace even at first glance or sight?
Is it just the sound of a person's voice or the scent of their fragrance?
Is like a walk on the beach or like a flutter of a butterfly's wings?
Is it like a meeting of the minds over a long conversation?
Is it as fine as a glass of aged wine or can it be defined throughout the test of time?
Is it as gentle as calming wave that rolls into shore or is it as rough as a hurricane?
Is it like math an exact science or like good literature an array of endless possibilities?
The solution for sure doesn't rely on what is between your thighs or below the waist but it's a play with fate in what's at stake like mutual respect and the foundation of a profound friendship
Oh well I guess it's safe to say the rules are set by the players at the table and if the cards are dealt right or maybe it's like war easy to start but hard to finish

Chapter 2

Hope

Webster's dictionary defines hope in wanting something to happen and think it could happen or be true. I think hope and faith play hand in hand, in God as well as encompassing your being and what goes on around you in the world. Contrary to popular belief we sometimes have to be careful what we hope for and sometimes what we hope for we don't always get. That's probably because God is trying to protect us from hurt and disaster. He may also be stirring us in a better direction which can lead to fulfilling our true purpose. He will give us the desires of our heart but it must be according to his will. I had to come to this conclusion myself after bumping my head up against a wall or going down a dead end road. In my stubbornness I discovered that God's plan for my life is always what's best for me. As a matter of fact there are times when he may not reveal his plan to me, but I just have to walk in obedience unto him. People I know you are saying that is one of the hardest things to do. Yes, it can be at times but it's better than following man's plan for your life. God does place

certain people in our lives to fulfill his will and purpose but we must be very careful who we associate with. This is when we must use wisdom and the spirit of **discernment** to make good choices.

Life

- In life I've learned that you can gain knowledge from the insignificant to the significant nature of people
- In life I've learned that your failures make you strong and not weak
- In life I've learned that your past or present doesn't have to dictate your future destiny and that's why it's called the present
- In life I've learned that complaining & whining does nothing but pollute your spirit plus creates stumbling blocks in one's life
- In life I've learned that you must cherish the folks that love you because they are your cheerleaders in life's journey
- In life I've learned that sometimes silence is the best defense rather than a comeback line
- In life I've learned that we all make mistakes and we must not beat up on others or ourselves
- In life I've learned that some paths are meant to be walked alone
- In life I've learned that the people closest to you can hurt you the most
- In life I've learned that the company you keep can make or break you
- In life I've learned that love is a beautiful thing but it can sometimes hurt

- I've learned that God never changes, people do and he still performs miracles, but we must sit still in order to recognize them
- Life is full of lessons don't sleep through its sessions or lessons cause you could be missing out on its many blessings

When We Remembered

- When we remembered little ones weren't playing in the streets till 1am in the mourning
- When we remembered little girls jumped double Dutch and shake pompoms & not sheet
- When we remembered young people respected & paid homage to their elders plus they didn't treat them like chatter boxes or with disrespect. They really are and have been pearls of wisdom whose voices echo throughout timeless generations.
- When we remembered we were a people of color who embraced one another with peace signs, slaps of five on the hand, & we made strong music like rhythmic bands
- When we remembered Mama's spent time nourishing and guiding their children with strong moral foundations. They weren't out chasing men at clubs or bumping & grinding till the early mourn
- When we remembered real men were head of the households and there were fewer single moms
- When we remembered corner stores, plus five & dimes were ours and not folks from foreign lands who treat us like we got dirty hands
- When we remembered fewer brothas & sistas for that matter were behind bars and more were writing books cause education was a major priority
- When we remembered preachers in church weren't masquerading as Politian's, businessmen, or crooks because they were more concerned about the true foundations that are in the good book

- When we remembered people gave God their time, he in return gave them peace of mind
- Now we have forgotten our ancestry cause we got so much more but give so little to our mission and plight
- We have sold out our youth who have become hopeless because we dropped the ball from a terrible fall from grace all cause we forgot to instill the teachings of our race

Anyway

- When I walk in the office place and speak folks don't acknowledge you smile and keep shining anyway
- When certain family members treat you like an outcast or freak of nature love & pray them anyway but from afar, cause up close could interrupt your peace of mind
- When your kids are acting like mis-fits or Be-Be kids do less of going upside their heads, instead anoint them, pray, be patient, and watch God turn the situation around anyway
- When you run into your ex who broke your heart into bits/pieces look your best; say hello and keep it moving in the other direction anyway
- When young people in your neighborhood dress like thugs/strippers don't be nasty toward them, but tell them that it looks better to be classy rather than trashy and to dress for success. You'll get taken seriously with respect and love the hell of them anyway
- When your mind is heavy and you don't know if you're coming or going just stand and call on the name of Jesus anyway. Watch how calm your spirit becomes there is peace in his name.
- In spite of my problems and life's ever changing circumstances I will keep praising God anyway. Although at times I'm turned upside down, don't know if I'm coming or going, I know for sure Jesus is able, stable and available to us all anyway.

Hope In A Time of Hidden Agendas

In today's society people are not what they appear to be. They wear many different masks on any given day. They switch up on you more than the weather or a chameleon's array of colors. They have hidden agendas and sneaky motives to devour you as soon as your back is turned. They smile in your face while all along plotting for your disgrace or scheme for a down fall. I am finding it less than more in coming across people who are genuine and not complicated or phony to deal with. Whatever happened to the days when folks were compassionate, ethical and true to heart. I'm feeling and seeing people in the world shifting in a negative gear instead of a positive gear. Grand Master Flash and the Furious Five a rap group, put a rap song out in 1982 called "The Message". The rap's chorus stated "It's like a jungle sometimes it makes me wonder how I keep from going under, don't push me cause I'm close to the edge, I'm trying not to lose my head". These lyrics echo the pain and pressure of just what's going on mentally in today's society. Most of the leaders of today don't address or hear the cries of people who are down trotted. Their greed and love for money plus power come first not the poor or destitute. What's good is looked at as bad. Corruption is running rampant. They are moving and thinking backwards rather than forward. Leaders from back in the day looked out for the interest of others. They were also visionaries who created blue prints which were constructed for future generations. This type of structure escalated a foundation of growth and not destruction. Parents were more equipped as well as now. They are allowing their kids to raise themselves

or they're committing more abuse at a higher level. Children aren't respecting adults nor are afraid of seen of unforeseen consequences. I guess the human race can only be saved by God and those who are standing up for righteousness that God uses as his vessels of miraculous power.

Hidden agendas are always revealed when the light is shed on the darkness. The unseen becomes visible in time. Hope can reflect one's inner courage. It's God given in times of adversity. Hope is **(Having Ongoing Possibilities and Expectations).** When all seems lost we must keep hope ignited it can be used to light our pathway to a better tomorrow.

Chapter 3

Faith

Faith is a strong belief or trust in something or someone. It's also a system of religious beliefs based on the existence of God. Spiritually faith is the substance of things hoped for but not seen and it's the essence of all things that life encompasses. Faith to me is like stepping outside feeling & seeing how the wind blows the trees. You can't see the wind with your man's eye but you can see it exist plus you feel it against your skin. That's how faith in God works, but I see his works in the sky, change of weather, nature's water ways, and its beautiful landscapes. Not to mention the evolution of man and having God blow breath into our bodies from day to day. Faith is what sustains me from day to day and at times from moment to moment. It allows me to face my fears with courage in knowing that God is the wind beneath my feet. He carries me when I'm weary and gives me the strength to endure life's adversity. I challenge you to make it on your own aside from him and see how far you go the distance. If you do it's not coming from God but the devil. He can at times send fake favor or blessings. True blessings come from God because it

includes joy & not happiness. Happiness is an emotion but joy comes only from God. The devil is famous for deceiving and he is the King of deception. He can make something look good when it's not. He comes to steal, kill, & destroy. At times become prey to his tactics because we get weak.

Many of us choose to do things our way rather than wait on the Lord because of lack of patience. I can testify to that but now I've learned the importance of trusting, waiting on God, and having complete faith in him. There are many lessons before the blessings. Besides when you wait on God he sends you more than you could ever imagine plus he gives you peace of mind. Peace is priceless and free. Faith can turn what seems impossible into the possible.

Never Give Up

- Life is what you make it of course there are high and low points
- Its like a roller coaster ride full of twists and turns called disappointment that can be heart breakers or life changers
- They can also be God's way of steering us in a different direction like caution signs or dead ends on a street
- There are some folk who never seem to bounce back
- I say never give up even when you see no light don't choose to be a complainer or toxic, these are weapons of mass destruction
- Never give up
- Choose the high roads of life
- Embrace love, peace, and joy these three can raise your spirit from within and be a comfort in bad times when faith is mixed in
- Never give up just dust yourself off and change your way of thinking instead
- Start today and say to yourself I must be complete rather than deplete in order to progress in this journey called life
- If you quit you will never see what's on the other side of the storm or meet God's path which could lead to your destiny
- The road had to be bumpy in order to be about strength and wisdom that builds character
- Never give up

- Never stop reaching, teaching, or giving up especially not with yourself
- Never give up your dreams for they can become your reality if you don't doubt your morality

Jesus

- Who was the only person God sent in the form of man to heal the entire land? –Jesus-
- Who is the only man that truly understands your pain? –Jesus-
- Who sits at the throne of the right hand our father God? –Jesus-
- Who died for all of our sins, so that we may have true life? –Jesus-
- Who is the only man that died and rose again from the dead? It wasn't Budda or any other idol. It was Jesus!!!
- Who is a combination of a comforter, friend, plus problem solver all in one form? –Jesus-
- Whose name holds power when spoken that causes the devil and demons on every level to tremble or flee? –Jesus-
- Jesus is the way, the truth, and the light that sustains throughout any fight cause he holds all might and power that's higher than any tower
- Choose him today cause he's the only way

Angels

- Are angels just in heaven or do they walk among us on earth?
- Do they have wings to soar high above the clouds and throughout the atmosphere?
- Do angels have a particular rank or level in heaven? Does God appoint them according to their specialty?
- One things for sure is that they are spiritual beings who triumph over evil demons who are filthy heathens
- They are messengers from God who are appointed to guard over and protect human beings
- They keep us safe and deliver messages of escape from dangerous zones
- I feel as though babies and children are angels because they have pure hearts which haven't been tainted yet
- I feel as though friends and loved ones are angel like who serve with love and care. They also have time to spare in being there when one is in despair.
- I know for certain that you shouldn't sleep on or judge a stranger who comes across your path, you could be entertaining a angel sent by God.
- Keep your heart and eyes open to those who appear strange for they maybe an angel in disguise with a blessing wrapped up in a weird dressing.
- Angels come in all shapes, sizes, and appearances, so don't bury your head in the sand when a special man approaches you. God could be testing your heart to see if you could play a beautiful spiritual Godly part called humility.

Only a Prayer Away

- Just know you're only a prayer away have faith that God is right there listening and answering your prayers. Because he's carrying you through the darkness of life, so you can walk into the precious light. –God's only a prayer away
- When you're faced with all kinds of famines from financial ruin to relationships with others, you may think the pain will never end. These are the times you must take a moment to reflect on your past and current blessings. –God's only a prayer away
- Allow your mind and spirit to flow on the present day to take time out to pray-God's only a prayer away
- When your so call family and friends abandon you God will replace them with his love. He will call on his angels to surround you with protection.
- Just talk to him, it's when you think he's asleep that he does his best work and that's when he's carrying you- God's only a prayer away
- He will take you by surprise and show up in another disguise. That's part of his mystery, but you can't take him in with your mind, you must absorb him with your spirit instead by reading his word. Use this as your weapon to slay the devil. This will defeat him in his games of tricks and deception-God's only a prayer away
- God is right there in the fight collecting all of your tears, fears, pain, and strain cause he's only a prayer away

- ➢ Continue to fight on bended knees asking God to show you the way from the valley to the mountain high. You will soon feel like you can touch the sky and fly like a beautiful butterfly. Cause God's only a prayer away!!!!

Scriptural References

1. Love: (Conquers All) 1 Corinthians 13, 1Corinthians 14:4-8,13; John 13:33-35; Proverbs 13:24; and John 1:15
2. Hope: (Reflects our Inner Courage) Mark 5:35-36; Luke 18:35-43; 1Corthians 15:54-56; Philippians 3:13-14; and Hebrew 6
3. Faith: (Is the Essence of All Things) Luke 18:35-43; Genesis 12:10; Genesis 15:6; and 2Kings 6:16

Edwards Brothers Malloy
Oxnard, CA USA
March 8, 2016